FEEDER BIRDS

OF EASTERN NORTH AMERICA

FEEDER BIRDS

OF EASTERN NORTH AMERICA

*Getting to Know Easy-to-Attract
Backyard Visitors*

SANDY ALLISON

featuring illustrations by AMELIA HANSEN

STACKPOLE
BOOKS

Copyright © 2014 by Stackpole Books
Illustrations copyright © 2014 by Amelia Hansen

Published by
STACKPOLE BOOKS
5067 Ritter Road
Mechanicsburg, PA 17055
www.stackpolebooks.com

Printed in the United States of America

10 9 8 7 6 5 4 3 2 1

First edition

Library of Congress Cataloging-in-Publication Data

Allison, Sandy, author.
    Feeder birds of eastern North America : getting to know easy-to-attract backyard visitors / Sandy Allison ; featuring illustrations by Amelia Hansen. — First edition.
        pages cm
    ISBN 978-0-8117-1223-1
    1. Birds—East (U.S.)—Identification. 2. Birds—Canada, Eastern—Identification. I. Hansen, Amelia, illustrator. II. Title.
QL683.E27A45 2014
598.097—dc23
                                                                2013031710

CONTENTS

FAMILIAR FRIENDS

Bird-watchers know there is a list of species that regularly and dependably come to dine at backyard bird feeders. These are the "feeder birds," the group bird-watchers are most familiar with, and the group that probably got them interested in birds in the first place. Feeder birds are a diverse lot, but they have a few things in common—most importantly, they are adapted to eat seeds or suet and are unafraid to frequent places where people live.

Like most animals, most birds eat only certain items and live in specific environments. Warblers, for instance, feed on caterpillars, beetles, moths, and tiny insects—and many warblers eat this diet only in the tops of tall trees. The American woodcock feeds mainly on earthworms, using a long, sensitive bill to find them in loose soil. It is highly unlikely you will ever see a woodcock (or even a warbler, for that matter) snatch a sunflower seed from a feeder no matter how hungry it might be.

But you *will* see chickadees take seeds, and doves, and cardinals, and nuthatches, and finches. In fact, you might very well see every feeder bird covered in this book at your feeder at least once—if you keep the feeder full, and if you are watching. Being able to identify these familiar birds at a glance, and learning their habits, quirks, and behaviors, will add to your enjoyment of these species—and other species—immensely.

HOUSE SPARROW

Passer domesticus

A distinctive black chin helps you identify the male house sparrow, likely the most common North American feeder bird.

The house sparrow will probably be the first visitor to your newly installed feeder and the most frequent visitor over the years. These noisy brown birds have adapted to almost every environment you can think of—they can be found in courtyards, parking lots, playgrounds, shopping plazas, flower gardens, and city streets—and in backyards big and small. The only place they aren't found is in the deep forest or desert.

The birds build their nests in the nooks and crannies of trees, fences, and buildings—they seem especially partial to walls draped with thick ivy. They sometimes raise three different broods in one year, or a total of six or seven youngsters. Besides birdseed, house sparrows eat flower buds, insects, weed seeds, and garbage. At a feeder, they are prone to squabbling.

Male house sparrows have distinctive black chins and gray caps. Females are a nondescript grayish brown with no distinct markings.

House sparrows are more closely related to European sparrows than they are to the other sparrows that visit your feeder, such as chipping sparrows or song sparrows. And unlike those visitors, house sparrows aren't native to North America. They arrived in the 1850s, after being introduced from England, which is why they were once known as English sparrows. Today, there are few places in the world that aren't home to house sparrows (even if they're called something else). In fact, they are the most numerous species of bird on the planet.

Small flocks of house sparrows will visit the feeder itself or gather on the ground to eat what's been dropped or spilled.

HOUSE FINCH

Carpodacus mexicanus

The male house finch has a wash of reddish-purple on its head, face, and chest.

The house finch once had a limited range in this country—until 1939, when a few California birds were released in New York City. Since then, the house finch population has exploded, and the species is common throughout most of the country (including Hawaii, where it's nicknamed the "papaya bird" in honor of its favorite food). And the bird seems to prefer to live near humans and human habitations, commonly building its nest on buildings and other man-made structures. If the house sparrow is the most frequent feeding station visitor, the house finch is a close second.

Female house finches are grayer than female house sparrows—both are nondescript, however, especially compared with the males.

Both male and female house finches are streaky brownish-gray overall. Males have reddish or raspberry coloring on their heads, faces, and chests. Females, without this coloring, are sometimes confused with sparrows, but they are generally grayer than those species.

House finches have a pleasant twittering song. Although some house finches migrate, scientists are not sure just how many, or exactly how far they travel. Most house finches, it seems, are year-round residents. You'll likely get to know them quite well.

PURPLE FINCH

Carpodacus purpureus

Male purple finches have been described as looking as though they've been dunked in cranberry juice.

Often confused with the house finch, the purple finch is much less common in its range. When you're trying to identify a reddish feeder finch, it's wisest to think house finch first then look closely to see if it might actually be a purple finch. Like male house finches, male purple finches have raspberry coloring on their heads, faces, and chests, but they also have it down their backs—they are *very* reddish instead of just *kind of* reddish. They also have plainer, whiter breasts, and their gray-brown coloring is slightly more brown than gray.

Female purple finches don't have any red, but they have plainer heads and backs than do female house finches. Even as house finch populations are increasing, purple finches are in decline. This is likely because they compete—unsuccessfully, it seems—with their more-widespread relatives.

Purple finches are migrants and so are seen across much of the southeastern United States only in winter. They are welcome feeder visitors but notoriously inconsistent. In some winters, they will be quite common; in others, they will not show up at all. In the Northeast, they are year-round residents. In stretches of eastern Canada, they are found only during breeding season. On their northerly breeding grounds, purple finches build their nests most often in pine, fir, or spruce trees.

The female purple finch has a plain appearance, without the namesake coloration.

AMERICAN GOLDFINCH

Carduelis tristis

The male goldfinch's vivid "spring" plumage lasts through the summer; the species is one of the latest to nest.

Watch a goldfinch fly and you will see a definite bounce. This illustrates how some birds flap for a bit then glide, flap for a bit then glide—when they flap, they gain altitude; when the glide, they drop lower—causing an undulating flight. The American goldfinch sometimes adds a bouncy twittering call, making it a distinctive backyard visitor.

Goldfinches love thistle seeds and will flock to a well-stocked thistle feeder. In the nesting season, they also occasionally eat small insects. They use the down from thistle plants to line their tightly woven nests. The species lays its eggs later in the year than any other feeder bird, often as late as August.

Many parts of North America have goldfinches all year, although the birds form large flocks and wander widely in search of food during the winter. During this period, the male's vivid yellow plumage fades to a dull olive color, and the bird can be difficult to identify.

The American goldfinch is distinct from the widespread European goldfinch, which is somewhat similar but has red markings on its face. The European species makes an appearance in the United States only as part of Pennsylvania Dutch folk art—it's known as the *distlefink* (or "thistle finch") and is a traditional German motif.

American goldfinches are just as active, although not as noticeable, in winter as they are in summer.

BLUE JAY

Cyanocitta cristata

The big, beautiful blue jay is one of the most familiar birds in North America. Loud and aggressive, the bird lives year-round throughout the central and eastern United States and southern Canada. It does not migrate.

The blue jay screams a strident *jeee!* or *jaay!* that resounds through the neighborhood. It also makes somewhat odd, liquid-sounding *wheedle-ee* or *clee-op* calls, which at first don't seem to emanate from a bird. But if you can spot what's making this noise, you'll see the blue jay, bobbing its head. Blue jays also do a mean imitation of a red-tailed and red-shouldered hawk.

Like related crows and ravens, jays seem to be smart. They've been observed using tools to help them obtain food. They've also been known to startle smaller birds into dropping their meal so the jay can swoop in and steal it. They eat a widely varied diet: seeds, nuts, acorns, fruit, beetles,

Blue jays have been widely studied and are believed to be one of the most intelligent bird species.

The blue jay's plumage features a striking pattern of varied blues mixed with black and white.

wasps, dragonflies, and small vertebrate animals, including bats and frogs. They'll also eagerly eat dog food and bread left out by humans.

Blue jays seem to thrive in and around man-made environments. Typically a bird of leafy or evergreen forests, some studies have noted that they nest more often in lightly wooded suburban habitats than in less-disturbed landscapes.

NORTHERN CARDINAL

Cardinalis cardinalis

Unlike most bird species, which molt into duller plumage for the winter, the male cardinal retains its bright red color throughout the year.

What makes male cardinals so red? It's their food. A certain pigment in the items they eat (called a carotenoid) isn't synthesized during digestion and so is deposited in their feathers. Scientists believe that the quality of the male cardinal's diet affects the brightness of its feathers, which in turn helps it attract a mate.

Cardinals are now common throughout much of the country, but this wasn't always the case. In the mid-1800s, they were rarely, if ever, seen north of the Ohio River. And it wasn't until the 1940s and '50s that they became numerous in the Northeast. The birds don't migrate: in fact, scientists believe they spend their entire lives in a relatively small area.

Cardinals begin building their first nest of the season in March or April (sometimes even February). Tangled thickets or dense shrubs are favorite sites. The pair will often attempt to nest three, four, even five times a year, although usually only one or two of these tries is successful. They build a new nest each time.

You'll quickly learn to recognize the northern cardinal's song: a melodic, sliding *whit-cheer, whit-cheer, wit, wit, wit* or clear *purdy, purdy, purdy.* It also makes a loud, metallic-sounding *chip!*

The female northern cardinal is mainly brownish with hints of red on its head and wings.

TUFTED TITMOUSE

Baeolophus bicolor

Titmice, along with cardinals and chickadees, are frequent visitors to a well-stocked wintertime feeder.

This favorite feeder bird is a common fall and winter visitor, and it will make good use of the food you provide. Tufted titmice are known to snatch a morsel (usually the largest sunflower seed available) and fly away, and if they don't hammer it open and eat it immediately, they store the unshelled seed in a crevice in the bark of a nearby tree or other hiding place, creating a cache of food they can raid when food is scarce. Scientists believe they build up a number of such caches in different spots within their territory.

Male and female titmice look the same, but it's the male that does the singing. Its song is a loud and insistent *peer-peer-peer,* made repeatedly in the spring from a prominent perch. Although the tufted titmouse doesn't migrate, it is seen at the feeder much more frequently during the colder months. And the titmice at a feeder in the winter might be a family. After fledging, juvenile titmice sometimes remain with their parents throughout the first year of their lives—which is fairly unusual in most bird species.

The tufted titmouse eats insects and caterpillars more than it does seeds, but that doesn't prevent it from regularly feasting at the feeder. Like its frequent companion the chickadee, the titmouse makes a raucous call when it's upset.

The tufted titmouse is now widespread throughout most of the eastern United States. Studies in the 1970s showed that its range is spreading northward, probably because of habitat change, the increased availability of food from feeders, and global warming.

The tufted titmouse will typically hold a morsel of food with its feet and hammer it open with its bill.

CAROLINA CHICKADEE

Poecile carolinensis

Carolina chickadees seem to have a neat appearance, with precise edges to their markings.

It's difficult for even experienced birders to tell the difference between a Carolina chickadee and a black-capped chickadee just by looking at them. One of the best ways to identify them is to check their range maps—there are relatively few parts of the country that are home to both species. You can also learn their songs. If you're lucky enough to hear them sing, you'll know that *fee-bee, fee-bay* means a Carolina chickadee and *fee-bee* or *fee-bee-bee* means a black-capped.

Both kinds of chickadees eagerly take food from feeders. They'll snatch a seed, fly to a nearby perch, hammer the seed

BLACK-CAPPED CHICKADEE

Poecile atricapillus

The black-capped chickadee is slightly larger and scruffier than the Carolina chickadee. Both are equally acrobatic.

open with their bill, gulp the kernel down, then return for another meal. They also readily eat from suet feeders. They often raise a ruckus during mealtime, scolding birds and other intruders and making sure everyone knows they're around. In the winter, chickadees flock up with other species, especially titmice and

When alarmed, the chickadee will raise the crest of feathers on the top of its head.

nuthatches (which also visit feeders) as well as kinglets and warblers (which don't). More birds mean more eyes to spot food and scan for predators.

Many birds are small, but chickadees are especially tiny, weighing no more than half an ounce. To survive freezing winters, chickadees store seeds in the crevices of trees and under dead leaves and elsewhere, stockpiling sustenance for when food is scarce. They also can lower their body temperature by some fifteen degrees, reaching a state of controlled hypothermia to help conserve precious calories.

BLACK-CAPPED OR CAROLINA?
In general, the black-capped chickadee's range includes southern Canada, New England, New York, northern New Jersey, and

much of Pennsylvania. It includes Michigan and the northern-most portions of Ohio and Indiana. The black-capped chickadee also lives in the higher elevations of the Appalachian Mountains in West Virginia.

The Carolina chickadee's range extends from southern New Jersey, Pennsylvania, and Maryland through Virginia to cover all of the South to mid-Florida. It includes most of Ohio and Indiana and all of Tennessee, Kentucky, Mississippi, and Alabama.

The two species' ranges overlap only in parts of New Jersey, Maryland, Pennsylvania, West Virginia, Ohio, and Indiana.

Chickadees are noisy and assertive: the bird's buzzy *chicka-dee-dee-dee* call enlivens a backyard feeding station.

WHITE-BREASTED NUTHATCH

Sitta carolinensis

Although they are especially attracted to suet feeders, nuthatches will also take seeds from a seed feeder.

Although they won't do it at the feeder, white-breasted nuthatches will demonstrate a fairly unique ability on trees: they are one of the very few bird species able to move headfirst down a trunk. Two adaptations help them accomplish this—their feet are placed relatively far apart, and their tail is not structured for use as a brace, as is that of other tree-trunk foragers. The bird's typical pose is to cling vertically along a tree trunk, tail above head, which is often held horizontally so the bird can scan its surroundings.

Nuthatches are widespread throughout the eastern United States; they like thinly wooded areas or ones that are near open areas. Eastern white-breasted nuthatches do not migrate and can be seen year-round within their range. Listen for their distinctive *yank, yank* call.

Like many woodpeckers, white-breasted nuthatches build their nests in tree cavities. But they don't dig them out themselves; instead, they use old woodpecker cavities or other holes in tree trunks and limbs, where the female builds a nest before laying its eggs.

The white-breasted nuthatch can often be seen scampering down tree trunks while searching for food.

RED-BREASTED NUTHATCH

Sitta canadensis

Smaller than a white-breasted nuthatch, and with bold black-and-white stripes on its head (as well as a reddish belly instead of white), this feeder bird is resident of Canada and the northern states, as well as New York, Pennsylvania, and the Appalachian Mountains. But because it can and often does travel widely in the winter, it can make an appearance almost anywhere in the eastern part of the country. Experts believe this irregular

The red-breasted nuthatch is a tiny jewel-like bird that makes irregular visits to backyard feeders.

Like the white-breasted nuthatch, the red-breasted nuthatch is adept at moving headfirst down trees.

and unpredictable southward movement is connected with a lack of food on the home range to the north.

This nuthatch is small but it's loud, with a characteristic call often described as sounding like the bleat from a tiny tin horn. Like other nuthatches, the red-breasted nuthatch can walk head-first down the trunks of trees. It also makes quick flights from one perch to another. It nests in old woodpecker holes or other cavi-ties, often in dead or dying trees.

At one time, the red-breasted nuthatch was known as both the Canada nuthatch and the red-bellied nuthatch.

DARK-EYED JUNCO

Junco hyemalis

Although it is "dark eyed," the junco sports a conspicuous white belly that contrasts with its otherwise overall gray plumage.

These are the "snow birds" that seem to show up in the backyard at the start of winter and then leave as spring arrives. So where do they spend the rest of year? For the most part, across Canada. The middle latitudes of the United States is where their southern migration ends (in the Appalachian Mountains, New York, and across New England, these birds are year-round residents). You'll also see them on the ground in clearings during a walk in the woods. In flight, they flash white outer tail feathers.

An overall gray with a white belly and light-colored bill, juncos are almost always beneath the feeder, eating what other birds have dropped or poking through the mulch. In winter, they make a pretty twittering call.

The subspecies of dark-eyed junco that lives in the eastern part of the country is known as the "slate-colored" junco. A number of subspecies live in the West. They all look fairly unique—but they're all considered dark-eyed juncos (at least they are now; they were at one time classified as separate species).

Male and female juncos look very much alike, although the females are sometimes a little browner or lighter in color.

The junco most often feeds on the ground, eating what others have dropped.

MOURNING DOVE

Zenaida macroura

The female mourning dove broods its chicks in a flimsy nest, often built on the ground, or in very low branches of bushes and shrubs.

The high-pitched twittering the mourning dove makes when it quickly lands or takes flight is made by air flowing over its wings. It's not a vocalization. Both males and female doves coo, but the sad cooing that gives this bird its name is made by the male in an attempt to attract a mate. Most of this cooing occurs in the morning but can go on all day.

The mourning dove is one of North America's most common species. It ranges across most of the country and Mexico and in parts of Canada. The dove migrates to varying extents. Its life span is short: most adults live for only one year. The doves are widely hunted—many states currently allow the shooting of mourning doves in season.

The doves feed almost exclusively on seeds, and while they will sometimes perch on feeders, they usually pick at food on the ground. They nest on the ground, too, but also in shrubs and trees. After pairing up, during which the potential mates nuzzle together and preen each other, the female lays two eggs in a fairly flimsily constructed nest. Like many baby birds, newborn mourning doves are helpless and entirely dependent on adult care. They grow quickly, however, usually leaving the nest in a matter of weeks.

Although generally a uniform
olive-brown, the plumage of the mourning
dove reveals a subtle pink coloration.

DOWNY WOODPECKER

Picoides pubescens

The female downy lacks red on its head. The bristles at the base of the bill help protect the bird from flying wood chips as it hammers.

Our smallest woodpecker is the one that most commonly visits feeders, particularly if they contain suet or a suet-and-seed mixture. Both males and females sport a striking black-and-white feather pattern; males also have a red patch on the back of their head, which females lack. Scientists have also observed another distinct difference: males downies search for insects on smaller branches, either on low trees or high up in big trees; females hunt on large branches and the trunks of trees.

The downy lives year-round across most of the country and much of Canada in a variety of habitats, as long as they feature trees. The hairy woodpecker, which looks very similar to the downy, is more of a forest bird. It is less likely to show up in the yard. Hairy woodpeckers are a bit larger than downy woodpeckers, and they have longer bills.

Like other woodpeckers, downies make a drumming sound—usually a steady series of knocks that lasts a second or so and then is repeated. They also have the characteristic feet of woodpeckers, with two toes pointing forward and two pointing backward, which help them cling to the sloping surface of trunks and branches.

Listen for the downy's soft *pik* call and its horselike whinny.

The males of many species of woodpeckers have sharply contrasting black-and-white plumage accented with spots of bright color.

NORTHERN FLICKER

Colaptes auratus

The male "yellow-shafted" flicker sports a black mustache stripe.

This large woodpecker is a regular visitor to backyard feeders, but its favorite food is ants, which it searches for on the ground. Unlike most woodpeckers, which forage for food on tree trunks and branches, the flicker hops about earthbound, looking for colonies of ants and ant larvae, which it laps up with its tongue. It also eats beetles and seeds, but ants are definitely preferred.

The yellow shafts on eastern flickers are most visible when the bird spreads its wings.

The flicker does dig out cavities in dead trees and stubs for its nest, as do other woodpeckers. Experts are concerned that northern flicker populations seem to be in decline, perhaps because European starlings outcompete them for nesting holes. This trend is especially worrisome because many other species depend on flicker created cavities for their own nests.

The northern flicker has two distinct variations: a yellow-shafted and a red shafted version. Flickers in the eastern states are yellow-shafted. While male and female yellow-shafted flickers look the same, with a black bar across their chests and a red spot on the back of their heads, only the males sport a black "mustache stripe."

The northern flicker commonly makes a prolonged *wik-wik-wik-wik-wik* call or a single *keer*. It also drums on wood and other resonating surfaces at a rapid, steady pace.

RED-BELLIED WOODPECKER

Melanerpes carolinus

Red-bellied woodpeckers are unmistakable—their visits to feeding stations are a thrill.

It's a woodpecker that has red on its head, but it's not a red-headed woodpecker. It's a red-*bellied* woodpecker (there is red on the belly, but it can be hard to see). It's also just about the biggest bird that will visit your feeder. It's so big and boldly patterned that its sudden appearance can be startling.

Most red-bellied woodpeckers don't migrate, but when they're not nesting, they roam fairly widely in search of food. They aren't found in higher elevations. They are common in the southeastern part of the country, and their range is extending northward into New York and New England, in part because they have such a varied diet: seeds, fruit, berries, insects, even animals such as tree frogs and other, smaller birds.

Like most woodpeckers, red-bellied woodpeckers drum on hard surfaces to communicate, and they seem to choose things that will make the most noise, such as hollow limbs and metal roofs. Their drumming pattern is notably slower than that of other woodpeckers.

Their common call is a rolling *kwerr*. They also make lots of other calls—a variety of *churrs, chas,* and *chee-wucks*—throughout the year. They dig out holes in dead trees and fence posts to make their nests.

For the record: the red-headed woodpecker has an *entirely* red head and is unlikely to visit your feeder.

Although the red on the top and back of its head is most obvious, a close look reveals the reddish belly that gives the red-bellied woodpecker its name.

SONG SPARROW

Melospiza melodia

The song sparrow is likely the most common "true" sparrow that will visit your feeder.

L ook for the dark spot on the breast of this brown, streaky sparrow in order to identify it. Just about all eastern song sparrows have this marking. Male and females look the same. This is a common bird that ranges over most of the United States (even Alaska) as well as southern Canada and into Mexico. Scientists have identified dozens of subspecies that vary somewhat in appearance and behavior—but they're all song sparrows.

The male song sparrow usually sings from a highly visible perch.

True to its name, the species has a lovely song. Listen for two or three pure introductory notes that begin the musical phrase. You can imagine that the song sparrow "clears its throat" before it sings. And sing it does—males enthusiastically advertise their presence from prominent perches as breeding season begins. They sing throughout the day, but their most energetic performances are usually given early in the morning.

Although insects make up a big part of the song sparrow's diet, the bird readily visits feeders. Watch them on the ground making a quick little double hop, first forward then back, to uncover morsels that other ground feeders might have missed.

CHIPPING SPARROW

Spizella passerina

This small sparrow is named for its alarm call—a series of sharp *chips*. It also sings, but its song is a rather undistinguished trill, not very melodic. The chipping sparrow ranges throughout the eastern part of the country. Some birds migrate, breeding in the northern states and Canada, and some birds spend the winter in Florida. Many are resident all year in the rest of the range.

Chipping sparrows like to nest in shrubs and bushes near open areas; they are well suited to living in suburban neighborhoods. Scientists believe they are now more common in these settings than they are in undisturbed environments. Female chip-

Chipping sparrows are energetic feeder birds that spend much of their time on the ground.

Both male and female chipping sparrows have dark eye lines and reddish crowns.

ping sparrows test out possible nest sites before beginning to build. They perch in a likely spot and poke around at nearby nesting materials. Their nests are loosely assembled and look as though they might easily fall apart. Most chipping sparrow pairs nest twice in a season, building a new nest for each brood. Males can be unfaithful; they will sometimes breed with a couple different females during nesting season.

Chipping sparrows mostly feed on the ground. In the winter, they often visit feeders in small flocks. They are recognizable by their chestnut caps and dark eye lines, which fade in winter. They are relatively unstreaked, with light gray bellies.

WHITE-THROATED SPARROW

Zonotrichia albicollis

The white-throated sparrow has stripes on its head, as does the white-crowned sparrow, but its distinctive white throat patch makes it unique.

Similar at first glance to the house sparrow, this feeder bird has a stripy head and—you guessed it—a white throat, as well as a dot of yellow in front of each eye. Some birds have a whitish stripe above the eye; others have a tan stripe. Males and females look alike. It's a regular visitor during the winter, poking around on the ground for dropped seeds.

White-throated sparrows are common and widespread. They breed across much of Canada and spend the rest of the year throughout the eastern United States. They are one of a good number of birds known as "edge species," meaning they stay away from thick forests and wide-open areas, preferring habitats that are a mix of both—which is what much of the suburban landscape is. Because the birds are so numerous, scientists often use white-throated sparrows to study bird populations and the things that affect them.

Many older field guides describe this sparrow's song as "Old Sam Peabody," which implies that it consists of two longer notes following by three shorter ones. This was likely true at one time but is no longer the case. The sparrow is an active singer during breeding season, joining with other species to create a "dawn chorus" of birdsong in the hours just before sunrise.

Like many backyard birds, the white-throated sparrow prefers areas that have a mix of trees and open patches, typical of suburban neighborhoods.

WHITE-CROWNED SPARROW

Zonotrichia leucophrys

Migrating white-crowned sparrows make good use of the feeders they find on their winter grounds.

White-crowned sparrows are migrants. The birds that winter across much of the eastern United States (in all but the most northern states and Florida) breed in northern Quebec and Labrador. They generally arrive on their southern territories in the states in September and are gone by May. Scientists are studying exactly how these sparrows—and all migrating bird species—can manage to navigate such long distances twice a year. An

Look closely to see that the relative thicknesses of the white-crowned sparrow's head stripes are different from those of the white-throated sparrow.

innate ability to orient themselves with the lighting of the night sky seems to be a key factor.

Both male and female white-crowned sparrows sport a distinctive black and white cap and are easy to identify. They feed on the ground, scratching for food, which is mainly seed supplemented with fruits and insects.

White-crowned sparrows drink frequently. If you can provide ice-free water during the colder months, these sparrows (and many other birds) will especially appreciate the effort. As well, most sparrows will appreciate the shelter offered by a nice brush pile left in place through the winter.

AMERICAN TREE SPARROW

Spizella arborea

Despite the name, tree sparrows don't spend more time in trees than do most other bird species.

The name is somewhat misleading: the American tree sparrow shows no more fondness for trees than do most birds, and it spends only the colder months in the United States. The birds breed in the remote regions of upper Canada and Alaska. Apparently, early European settlers named the bird because they thought it looked like the Eurasian tree sparrow. All American tree sparrows migrate; the ones you see at your feeder spend the breeding season many, many miles to the north.

It's a small bird with a central breast spot, like the song sparrow, but it's not as streaky, especially on the chest, which is plain gray. It also sports a reddish cap. Males and females look alike. A common wintertime feeder bird throughout much of the northeastern part of the country, it usually travels in flocks.

Observers have seen this bird bat at the tops of tall weeds with its wings in order to dislodge seeds when the ground is covered with snow.

Different male tree sparrows sing similar but varied melodic songs. Each individual sings only one version. Females don't sing at all.

American tree sparrows often visit winter feeding stations in small flocks.

FOX SPARROW

Passerella iliaca

The fox sparrow has an overall patchy appearance, a mix of reds, grays, and browns.

Fox sparrows are large wintertime feeder visitors that will somewhat shyly poke through litter on the ground. They are a patchy reddish-brown and gray, with white bellies that are streaked and spotted. Their plumage can vary widely, however, depending on where you live. The bird you see in your yard might not look exactly like the image in your field guide. Fox sparrows will often scurry to cover when disturbed and so it's sometimes hard to get a good look.

The sparrows breed in Canada and are seen in the eastern states mainly in January and February, and into March. They eat both seeds and insects, scratching the ground with a hopping motion to help them find their food.

In the West, scientists have identified a number of different fox sparrow subgroups, with differences in behavior and plumages. In the East, their appearance is somewhat more consistent.

The fox sparrow's song is a pleasant twitter. Their population is believed to be stable, although scientists have difficulty studying nesting habits because the bird breeds in such remote areas. They do know that a parent will try to lure a predator away from a nest by pretending to have an injured wing, much as a killdeer does.

The fox sparrow generally visits eastern feeders only in the coldest months of January and February.

CAROLINA WREN

Thryothorus ludovicianus

Although its appearance is fairly conspicuous, the Carolina wren's ringing song helps you identify the bird even if you can't see it.

This large wren is distinctly reddish, with a warm cinnamon coloration above and a buff-colored belly. It also has a prominent white stripe above its eyes. The similar house wren is smaller and browner. Although its favorite food is insects and spiders, it will visit suet feeders and poke through the litter beneath a feeder.

Despite its name, the Carolina wren is found year-round throughout the eastern United States, except in the northern

The Carolina wren is the largest wren found in the eastern part of the country.

states. Its population is expanding northward, however, because of global warming and, perhaps, the increased presence of backyard feeding stations. In the South, this wren is a common sight, and its loud *tea-kettle, tea-kettle* song is a familiar sound.

The Carolina wren will build its nest inside all sorts of objects, including flowerpots, mailboxes, buckets, and watering cans. It sometimes incorporates feathers, strips of plastic, animal fur, even snake skins into the structure. It will occasionally raise three separate broods in a season—not in the same nest, but within the same territory, to which it is usually quite faithful.

Like a nuthatch or creeper, the Carolina wren will sometimes hitch itself up the trunk of a tree.

EASTERN TOWHEE

Pipilo erythrophthalmus

The female eastern towhee sports reddish flanks but is chocolate brown on top instead of black like the male.

At one time, the eastern towhee and the similar spotted towhee were considered one species: the rufous-sided towhee. They are now classified as two separate species. The outdated "rufous-sided" name came from the distinctive reddish flanks of both males and females. "Towhee" refers to one of the bird's common calls, also often described as *chee-link!* (its song is almost always rendered as "drink your tea!").

Classified as a type of sparrow, the eastern towhee spends almost all of its time on the ground, rooting through leaf litter for insects and seeds. To uncover such morsels, it scratches the ground with both feet, making a strong hop that tosses debris behind it. Such activity can make a mess of your mulch.

Ornithologists are troubled by the sharp decline in eastern towhee numbers noticed over the past decades. Reasons for the drop are unclear, but because the bird depends on extensive tree understory growth and thick leaf litter (it shuns both cleared areas and dense forests), it's believed that the disappearance of forest understory is affecting towhee populations.

The eastern towhee lives year-round throughout much of the eastern United States, although the mid-Atlantic, upper Midwest, and northern states may have only breeding populations that migrate south in colder months.

Male towhees sing from a "ground perch" a branch or rock or stem that elevates the bird ever so slightly above its immediate surroundings.

BROWN-HEADED COWBIRD

Molothrus ater

The cowbird is notorious as a "brood parasite": the female lays its eggs in the nest of another bird species, allowing the unwilling host to brood and raise the cowbird as if it were its own. This often doesn't work—the host may recognize the "new" egg and push it out of the nest. But it succeeds often enough for it to be a successful strategy for the cowbird to thrive, often at the expense of other species.

The list of species that serve as cowbird hosts is long and includes warblers, vireos, bluebirds, sparrows, phoebes, and many, many more. A few species (most notably the Kirtland's warbler) are in serious decline because of the cowbird's parasitic behavior.

Male cowbirds have an easily recognizable brown hood.

Female cowbirds are lightly streaked, like many other female species; its large beak helps identify it.

Male brown-headed cowbirds are easy to recognize. Females can look like sparrows and are a lightly streaked brownish gray. The species has a quick, high-pitched, tinkling song.

Cowbirds are named because of their habit of following cattle, which kick up the insects upon which the birds feast. They also eat seeds and almost always feed on the ground. A flock of cowbirds is referred to as a "herd" or "corral." Their year-round range covers just about all of the eastern United States.

EUROPEAN STARLING

Sturnus vulgaris

Most experts believe it's true: the entire North American population of European Starlings—an estimated 200 million birds—originated from a few dozen released in Central Park in the 1890s by a man who wanted to make sure that every bird mentioned by William Shakespeare was resident in the United States. It's likely one of the biggest avian population explosions in history.

Often confused with grackles, starlings are dark and speckled, sometimes somewhat shaggy, with yellow bills and pinkish legs (the bill is dark in winter). They can make an astonishing array of sounds: whistles, chatters, clicks, and whines, including a loud,

In spring, the starling's speckles and yellow bill distinguish it from the similarly colored grackle.

Starlings are noisy birds, especially when they gather in large flocks.

breathy *WHHEE-oo* that doesn't seem at all birdlike. In the fall, starlings sometimes form especially huge flocks.

As would be expected of a species that thrives over such a wide area, the European starling eats almost anything, including garbage. Experts have learned that its digestive system actually changes as the bird switches from eating plants to animals and vice versa.

Starlings are cavity nesters; the male usually begins building a nest before mating. Starlings often raise two broods a season, and an unattached female sometimes lays its eggs in a mated pair's nest.

COMMON GRACKLE

Quiscalus quiscula

The common grackle's bold yellow eyes set against dark, glossy plumage are distinctive.

This blackbird is sometimes confused with the European starling, but it has a sleek appearance, with iridescent purple-black or bronze-black plumage and distinctive yellow eyes. In flight, you will notice its wedge-shaped tail. It is a frequent backyard visitor, and it usually doesn't come alone. Grackles are known to gather in enormous flocks, especially during the fall and winter, when these groups (which include red-winged blackbirds, starlings, and other birds) can contain hundreds of thousands of birds.

The grackle eats seeds and insects, as well as large amounts of grain, which can be devastating to farms. It also pokes through garbage cans and dumpsites in search of man-made treats.

The species makes what is often referred to as a "squeaky hinge" call. Dozens or hundreds of squeaky grackles can raise quite a din. It also makes a distinctive *chek!*

The common grackle is widespread throughout the eastern United States, and its range is rapidly expanding to the West. It is at home in a variety of habitats, especially wetter areas, although it generally stays away from deep woods.

Scientists believe the grackle's "bill-pointing" behavior is a way for the bird to establish dominance.

EVENING GROSBEAK

Coccothraustes vespertinus

The evening grosbeak is an irregular visitor to wintertime feeding stations.

Flocks of this distinctive bird might visit your feeder during migration, but their arrival is unpredictable. While generally a year-round resident only in Canada, nests have been located in Massachusetts, Connecticut, Pennsylvania, and New Jersey. The evening grosbeak does travel, even if irregularly, throughout most of the eastern states.

The grosbeak's big, light-colored bill is its most recognizable feature. The bill allows the bird to get more nutrition from each seed it eats because it can often eat even large seeds whole. It also eats insects, especially certain types that inhabit trees.

Even though it's classified as a songbird, the evening grosbeak doesn't really seem to sing. Its common call is a single, rather flat, tweet. Because it's relatively reserved, even during breeding season, when many birds do all they can to get noticed, scientists have difficulty studying the species, and much is unknown about its life in the wild. The species' name is the result of an erroneous belief that the bird became vocal and active only as night approached.

Even though it lacks the male's striking markings, the female evening grosbeak can be recognized by its large bill.

COMMON REDPOLL

Carduelis flammea

Experts believe the redpoll's unpredictable movements are connected to the availability of certain tree seeds.

A feeder bird, but not a very common one—unless you're lucky. Common redpolls breed in remote northern Canada and regularly migrate south only to New England and New York. But in some years, and the timing is unpredictable, redpolls will head further south in large numbers, crowding feeding stations where they've never been before, and perhaps won't be seen again. Experts believe these erratic southern movements are connected to the failure of northern trees to produce adequate amounts of seed.

The redpoll's name refers to its red forehead markings: one of the meanings of *poll* is "top of the head."

Redpolls are small and active, flitting about and emitting a constant, rapid *che, che* call. They feed almost exclusively on small seeds, although they will eat insects during breeding season.

The common redpoll also lives in Europe and Asia, as well as Iceland. It's classified as a finch and is related to a number of other redpoll species.

PINE SISKIN

Carduelis pinus

In winter, the male pine siskin often sports brighter yellow markings than does the male goldfinch.

ook carefully at that flock of goldfinches crowding your thistle feeder in winter. If their plumage seems particularly streaky, with yellow highlights, they are likely pine siskins, an unusual winter visitor for much of the country that can, potentially, show up almost anywhere.

Like the common redpoll, the pine siskin appears well south of its regular range some winters and then might not be seen again for a very long time, if at all. It is what scientists call an "irruptive species." It breeds in the central parts of Canada and migrates south for the winter. But how far south it goes, and

Both male and female siskins appear very streaky, and they have thin, pointy bills.

when or exactly where it goes, is unpredictable and seems to be different every year.

Like the American goldfinch, the pine siskin feasts on tiny seeds, such as thistle. Its small, pointy bill is especially suited for this diet. In winter, it is likely to arrive in small flocks.

Pine siskins chatter as they feed. Their high-pitched calls include a distinctive steady buzz that ascends the scale, which some observers describe as a "watch-winding" sound.

SOURCES

The Birds of North America, published by the Cornell Lab of Ornithology and the American Ornithologists' Union, was the source of a number of facts in this book. This wonderful reference offers details on the natural history, habits, and habitats of every bird species native to the continent, gathered and written by scientists and other experts. The resource is accessible online, via subscription, at *bna.birds.cornell.edu/bna.* Larger libraries might have the print edition in their collections.

Photos courtesy of Shutterstock.com
Photo credits: p. 2, Andrew Williams; p. 4, Steve Brigman; p. 5, StevenRussellSmithPhotos; p. 6, Gregg Williams; p. 8, Nancy Bauer; p. 11, Gerald Marella; p. 12, Tom Reichner; p. 14, StevenRussellSmithPhotos; p. 16, Sari O'Neal; p. 17, Al Mueller; p. 18, LightShaper; p. 20, Ron Rowan Photography; p. 21, Bruce MacQueen; p. 23, Karel Gallas; p. 24, Steve Byland; p. 26, Lee Prince; p. 28, Paul Reeves Photography; p. 30, Elaine Davis; p. 31, Ron Rowan Photography; p. 32, Andrea J. Smith; p. 34, Michael Woodruff; p. 35, Stubblefield Photography; p. 37, Steve Byland; p. 38, Gerald Marella; p. 40, Keith Publicover; p. 41, Gerald Marella; p. 42, Steve Byland; p. 43, Tania Thomson; p. 44, Steve Byland; p. 46, Lorraine Hudgins; p. 47, StevenRussellSmithPhotos; p. 48, Visceral Image; p. 51, Steve Byland; p. 53, Reddogs; p. 54, Brian Lasenby; p. 56, Paul Reeves Photography; p. 57, Paul Reeves Photography; p. 58, Vitaly Ilyasov; p. 59, Kelly Nelson; p. 60, Kelly Nelson; p. 61, Jody Ann.

SIGHTINGS CHECKLIST

_____**House Sparrow** (male)
_____**House Sparrow** (female)
     *Notes:*_____

_____**House Finch** (male)
_____**House Finch** (female)
     *Notes:*_____

_____**Purple Finch** (male)
_____**Purple Finch** (female)
     *Notes:*_____

_____**American Goldfinch** (male)
_____**American Goldfinch** (female)

Notes: _____

_____

_____

_____

_____**Blue Jay** (adult)

Notes: _____

_____

_____

_____

_____**Northern Cardinal** (male)
_____**Northern Cardinal** (female)

Notes: _____

_____

_____

_____

_____**Tufted Titmouse** (adult)

Notes: _____

_____

_____

_____

_____**Carolina Chickadee** (adult)

Notes: _____

_____

_____

_____

_____**Black-capped Chickadee** (adult)

*Notes:*_____

_____

_____

_____

_____**White-breasted Nuthatch** (adult)

*Notes:*_____

_____

_____

_____

_____**Red-breasted Nuthatch** (adult)

*Notes:*_____

_____

_____

_____

_____**Dark-eyed Junco** (male)

_____**Dark-eyed Junco** (female)

*Notes:*_____

_____

_____

_____

_____**Mourning Dove** (adult)

*Notes:*_____

_____

_____

_____

_____**Downy Woodpecker** (male)
_____**Downy Woodpecker** (female)
      *Notes:*_____

_____

_____

_____

_____**Northern Flicker** (male)
_____**Northern Flicker** (female)
      *Notes:*_____

_____

_____

_____

_____**Red-bellied Woodpecker** (adult)
      *Notes:*_____

_____

_____

_____

_____**Song Sparrow** (adult)
      *Notes:*_____

_____

_____

_____

_____**Chipping Sparrow** (adult)
      *Notes:*_____

_____

_____

_____

_____**White-throated Sparrow** (adult)

_Notes:_____

_____

_____

_____

_____**White-crowned Sparrow** (adult)

_Notes:_____

_____

_____

_____

_____**American Tree Sparrow** (adult)

_Notes:_____

_____

_____

_____

_____**Fox Sparrow** (adult)

_Notes:_____

_____

_____

_____

_____**Carolina Wren** (adult)

_Notes:_____

_____

_____

_____

_____**Eastern Towhee** (male)
_____**Eastern Towhee** (female)

Notes: _____

_____

_____

_____

_____**Brown-headed Cowbird** (male)
_____**Brown-headed Cowbird** (female)

Notes: _____

_____

_____

_____

_____**European Starling** (adult)

Notes: _____

_____

_____

_____

_____**Common Grackle** (adult)

Notes: _____

_____

_____

_____

_____**Evening Grosbeak** (male)
_____**Evening Grosbeak** (female)

Notes: _____

_____

_____

_____

_____**Common Redpoll** (male)
_____**Common Redpoll** (female)

*Notes:*_____

_____

_____

_____

_____**Pine Siskin** (male)
_____**Pine Siskin** (female)

*Notes:*_____

_____

_____

_____